The Path to
Spiritual Growth
and Maturity

The Path to Spiritual Growth and Maturity

Solutions to Growing a Deeper Faith

Jerome,

I Hope The Book Will Be A Great Blessing.

J. Harris

Dr. J.A. Harris

CONTENTS

INTRODUCTION

At this point, you may be wondering if this book is worth it. I would like to ask some greater questions: "Are you ready for the spiritual journey?" and "Are you ready to break free from the spiritual institutionalization that has plagued our church communities for years?" It is time to grow and flourish in your quest for spiritual maturity. Prayerfully, you will not be the same after you read this book. However, I want you to do more than just read it. I want you to seek transformation and growth. I want you to process it in your soul and psyche. I desire that your inner person be changed. The book is designed to speak to your heart over the next eighteen chapters. I am not attacking anyone; I am only raising certain issues for the sake of spiritual growth.

The book includes a few of the spiritual disciplines as a way to lay a baseline for the faith. I hope you find the section on quiet time with God to be refreshing. There will also be chapters on discernment and surrender. Moreover, there is a chapter in the book on forgiveness—I hope you find it helpful.

In addition, sin is mentioned as a hindrance to spiritual growth. Fasting is covered in the midway chapters, along with study techniques. Make sure you check out the information on desiring God and growing through prayer. The toughest chapter may be the attempt to cover suffering as a redemptive measure of God. I wrote in simple words because Jesus used parables that everyone could understand.

I suggest that you read the book once and then read it again because it is a short book. In addition, please refer it to a friend because I believe that there is something for everyone within the content of this book. As you will come to find out, the chapters are short. This was done to keep you engaged. Also, let me say thanks for trusting me with your time and resources. I pray that the pages and topics will be of great benefit to you. I suggest that you say a quick prayer before embarking on each setting and each chapter—this approach will allow God to feed your spirit and soul. The prayer does not need to be extensive. It can simply be, "Lord, guide me through this reading and reveal your truth to me that will help me grow and mature for your Kingdom."

Finally, I would like to thank my wife and daughter for their support through this project and others. In addition, I am thankful for my church family at Roswell. I would like to send a special thanks to the proofreaders for their careful review of each line. Moreover, I would like to acknowledge my mom, grandmother, and godmother for their years of support. Also, I will give all credit to the Lord if even one life is enriched by the book.

01

Spiritual Growth / Spiritual Maturity

But grow in the grace and knowledge of our Lord and Savior Jesus Christ

– 2 PETER 3:18 ESV

Spiritual growth is a process. Yes, I know that sounds simple and I realize you may already know that. But the truth is the truth, it is a process. As a matter of fact, it is a long process where we surrender to God and allow His presence to rule and reign. The growth process encompasses the spiritual disciplines (study, prayer, meditation, worship, submission, confession, fasting, and silence) that lead to Spiritual Formation. Spiritual Formation is where we are being transformed into the image of Christ.

With that said, spiritual growth is a lifelong process that brings about spiritual maturity. Churches struggle with assisting new and existing members to reach their God-given potential because they may not have the proper discipleship systems in place to facilitate growth. Ultimately, the goal is to become Christlike (1 Corinthians 11:1). In the end, spiritual growth will require transformation (Romans 12:1-2). Transformation begins with the internal process of change that brings about fruit or external actions that reflect a transformed life. Spiritual growth similar to discipleship is a slow endeavor. The microwave approach will not cut it with individuals today. Spiritual growth is a slow process of developing a deeper relationship with Christ. This deep relationship continues to grow as the individual draws closer to Christ. Individuals will grow at different speeds, much of which will depend on the time invested in classes, life groups, individual study, prayer, worship, fasting, and mainly being in tune to the will and plan of God for each season of your life.

Spiritual growth will require community. We thrive in community. We experience accountability in community. We learn from others in healthy spiritual communities. As the old adage goes, "iron sharpens iron." Spiritual growth is desired by most Christians but attaining it is elusive. Spiritual growth evades us because we may not have fully surrendered to Christ or we have major sin ruling our thoughts and actions. God can use anyone at any time for His glory. However, He generally will use us in greater ways once we commit to the practice of growing on a daily basis. This practice is not the absence of sin because we all have missed the mark at some point (Romans 3:23). Growth is realizing that Satan wants us to sin by throwing things our way to distract us from reaching our goals. Spiritual growth will require a battle plan to defeat Satan (Ephesians 6:10). Growth is a measure of trusting the plans and process that God has laid out for each of us. The previous statement may seem contradictory because there is no easy fix for growing spiritually. I would avoid all plans that use the "lose-six-pounds-by-Friday" approach.

Again, it will take time. You will need to trust God in this process of growth and development. I am reminded by an earlier work from 1985 by Max Lucado titled *On the Anvil: Stories on Being Shaped into God's Image.* The work discusses how God has His own special process of how He changes us over time. God will need to shape and mold us for His glory. Better stated, we must allow God to shape and mold us for His glory.

Growth is also optional. In many cases, we are growing in the wrong areas. The systems at our houses of worship may only focus on the basics of doctrine. Yes, it is good to know the basics of Scripture. However, do you want more? Do you desire more? As a Christian, do you want to gain a deeper understanding of God? In the end, spiritual growth will require surrender and intentionality to a process that brings results. I challenge you to keep seeking and searching.

The next section will focus on spiritual maturity. In fact, we will compare spiritual growth to spiritual maturity. Spiritual maturity encompasses spiritual growth in that spiritual growth leads to spiritual maturity. Osmosis will not yield either result— it will take time and the presence of the divine Maker to get us to maturity. Spiritual maturity should be the ultimate goal for believers outside of making it to eternal glory. Maturing in your spiritual walk will take time and practice; it will also come with numerous mistakes. Mistakes or sin will serve as a reminder that we are not perfect in the sight of God.

Spiritual maturity often evades believers because we have improper measuring tools, like number of years in the faith, ability to quote Scripture, and ministry work. Spiritual maturity is living the Scriptures, not just quoting them. Maturity in Christ is not best judged by quantity of service, but by the quality of daily living. Paul, in Hebrews 6:1-2, promoted the idea of maturity or completeness. Paul makes a point to tell the believer to leave the elementary tenets of the faith and move onward to spiritual maturity.

The idea of "complete" or "mature" in the Greek language denotes being fully developed, moving forward in the process, reaching the end, and working through the stages. One idea may come from a mariner's perspective as they travelled by sea. The sea captain would fully extend his telescope to look further, to see land, to take an accurate reading of the stars. In the same way, we will not grow unless we allow ourselves to be fully extended toward Christ. The scope extends to see additional possibilities. The scope must be pointed in the right direction to see the best path to safety. Spiritual maturity combines teaching, coaching, and surrendering to see the bigger picture that God wants to show us. Spiritual maturity is acting on what we know by remaining disciplined through tough times. The mature Christian becomes reliant on the wisdom and divine knowledge of God. The spiritual wisdom overtakes our character over time and moves us further down the tracks, so to speak. Maturity in Christ is a process where we surrender all to Him because we wholly trust the process for our best life. Spiritual maturity is relying on God for directions. In some cases, spiritual maturity is waiting on God to deliver or being still and waiting for the proper next steps. Spiritual maturity is more concerned with application than information. Information is powerful, but application is doing and being. Spiritual maturity extends from a faith that believes that God knows best in every situation.

02

Quiet Time with God

Very early in the morning, while it was still dark, Jesus got up,
left the house and went to a solitary place, where he prayed

– MARK 1:35 NIV

Increasing in your faith is a daily task that requires consistent actions that connect you to Christ. Quiet time with God is one of the most important pieces of the puzzle because it incorporates praying, reading, meditation, and repenting. This list appears to be a modified grouping of the spiritual disciplines. The actions will serve as an avenue where we can be drawn closer to God. God ultimately wants our time, attention, and devotion. Quiet time is where we can tune into the presence of God. God knows we are too busy and overscheduled, and we are likely to forget to correspond with Him on a regular basis. This chapter is designed to help you determine the importance of spending quality time with your Holy Maker.

Time should be set aside each day to chat with God. This activity has the capacity to help us know or understand God on a deeper level. God wants our devotion; therefore, devotional time must be arranged on a daily basis if we are to truly know what God wants for us. I suggest that you carve out time in the early morning or before you retire for sleep. The mornings may coincide better with your schedule because you may not have been taxed with the activities of the day. Mornings are great because you are starting your day with godly communion time. In this case, I am not referring to the aspect of communion that requires us to take of His broken body and shed blood on Sunday (Acts 20:7). In fact, I am referring to a deeper meaning of the word that reminds us of the fellowship or bond we develop with God. Quiet time with God is essential to growing into the Christian that God wants us to become. The process of spending quiet time with God requires placing it on your schedule and making sure you stick to it in spite of challenges and circumstances. Again, quiet time is devotion to God where we pray, listen, ask questions, and seek advice from God that will allow us to keep on the path to spiritual maturity.

There is another usefulness for quiet time with God and it focuses on our obedience to His will. To make an earlier point, we are stretched, which makes spending quiet time with God more important. Conversely, the act of sacred time with God is obedience in the highest form because we make an internal declaration to put this practice into habit. Honestly, it will take time to develop this habit, but it will pay dividends in the long term. Simply stated, set a time to get up fifteen to twenty minutes earlier to read one passage while spending some time in prayer. Some people attempt to read one chapter before they get out of bed each morning. The process can include a focus on one biblical concept like faith, growth, or discernment. The rules are not etched in stone as to where the focus should be. The central thought is to make God the focus of your activities. Again, it will take time to develop this habit. However, I will almost guarantee that you will find immense benefits from this practice.

Quiet time is also a way to meditate on spiritual things to receive the best that God has to offer. Meditation is not just a practice for Eastern religions—it can and should be practiced by Christians today. Meditation cannot hurt you at all. In fact, the idea is developed from agriculture and farming. Please be advised, this next example may be kind of gross to your stomach. In farming, a cow will eat grass and "chew the cud" to gain vital nutrients. Remember, a cow has one stomach with four compartments. Therefore, a cow will digest the nutrients while chewing the grass. Within this process, the cow repeatedly takes the grass through the digestion process three or four times to gain more nutrients. Okay, I am trying to say it professionally. Let me put it this way. The cow eats the grass, takes it to its stomach, and then brings it back up time and time again to obtain additional nutrients with each regurgitation. This is the same way we should take in the Scripture—process it, think about it, think about it some more, and process it in our hearts again to get more spiritual nutrients. Just as the cow processes the grass three or four times to be filled and gain vital nourishment, we, also, should process the text numerous times to be spiritually filled.

Next, quiet time with God is also a way to frame your day. Beginnings are important because they start us in the right direction. If you have ever noticed any great Olympic sprinter, you will realize that starting is crucial. Starting your day with quiet time is essential. In some cases, quiet time can help you process through your important meetings or tasks you will be facing. Quiet time is prayer time, and prayer time is important. Praying is vital to the growth of a Christian because this is where we share our struggles with God. Prayer is also the place where we fight in spiritual warfare. Prayer will be discussed greater in a later chapter, but you must know the value of prayer—it serves to center your day because there will be distractions and critical situations that will test your spiritual competencies. Quiet time is essential for believers because it allows us to grow closer to God through a devotional process that draws God into our midst.

Yes, God is everywhere at the same time. But we are to call on Him throughout our day as a measure of showing our reliance on His power and presence. In the end, quiet time encourages you to turn everything over to your personal Higher Power.

03

Add to Your Faith

*Add to your faith virtue, to virtue knowledge,
and to knowledge self-control*

– 2 PETER 1:5-6 NKJV

Spiritual growth is not about knowledge only. It requires growing in the fashion of Christ in the areas listed in 2 Peter 1:5-7. As Christians, we should strive to be Christlike, which is the ultimate goal of all learning and transformation. The Scripture listed above reminds us that we should make every effort to add these necessary qualities to our spiritual clothing. The phrase "make every effort" (NIV) carries the idea of fully giving yourself to this cause or giving everything you have to accomplish this task. As disciples, we should give all that we have to become more spiritual. In the end, God will reward our obedience.

In another sense, we should go all out in the pursuit of spiritual maturity. Remember, before we can mature, we must grow. Peter is saying that we should give all that we have to grow in the likeness of our Savior. Peter goes further to say that we should add specific qualities to our spiritual walk. Adding encompasses the idea of increasing or gaining something. In addition, adding may also mean to place on or put on. The construct is to increase or grow in the areas that were named in the passage. The general idea is to add these positive attributes to your daily spiritual walk in an effort to grow for the sake of the Kingdom.

The first area mentioned is faith followed by goodness or virtue. The Christian should grow in the area of moral goodness, which is another way to say virtue. Virtue is listed in the New King James Version. However, I like the New Living Translation where it reads "moral excellence." I will use various translations to capture the new generation along with the super saints who have been in the faith for decades. Moral excellence, or virtue, is a state of doing things right for the right reasons. Moral excellence is a part of spiritual growth because, as Christians, we are expected to have virtue as an internal attribute that exudes outward to bring God glory. Moral excellence is a way of thinking that denies the flesh on a continual basis to allow the Christian the ability to mature and form in a spiritual manner more completely. In one way, this is where we surrender our natural thinking to become a more fully formed person of faith. The ancients did not think that moral excellence was an accident or happenstance—it was cultivated. Virtue is uprightness in our walk of faith toward God. It can be said that we are walking honestly before our Creator. An honest walk before God shows Him that we are trying to become better and that we are allowing the Holy Spirit to transform us on a second-to-second and minute-to-minute basis.

Next, knowledge is listed. I must warn you that this is not just learning the facts of the gospel—it is applying the facts of the gospel to our everyday walk. For instance, I have met a few Bible students over my lifetime who knew the Bible and could quote it quite well. However, they lacked a true knowledge of God. Let me say it this way, they had knowledge but not wisdom, they possessed an academic view of God, but lacked the experiential knowledge required to lead people or grow in their faith. Yes, they were growing in knowledge, but I am not sure they were growing closer to God. With that said, knowledge in this case on a deeper level leans on personal experience and firsthand information of His goodness and glorious ways. Yes, it includes the facts, but it also pulls in the total framework of His existence and character. Peter is referring to a knowledge that marries theory to real life application.

On another note, Peter was addressing the Gnostic cultures that existed in that day. Gnostics believed that knowledge of self exceeded everything. Hence, Peter in this passage talks about the real source of knowledge and the real reasons for knowing about Christ.

The Bible next mentions self-control. Self-control is not talked about in a lot of circles of faith today, but it is definitely needed by all believers, young and old. Self-control is to be added to your individual faith, like good moral living, knowledge, patient endurance, godliness, brotherly kindness, and love. Self-control will take you a long way as you seek spiritual growth and maturity. Self-control is not just the focus for youth groups, but all life groups in your church community. It is displaying mastery over something, and as Christians, we must continue to display mastery over sin if we are to grow and mature. Yes, we will fail from time to time. Better yet, we will fail daily as we miss the mark. On a deeper level, we are saying that we should be Spirit-controlled or Spirit-led. This may be new for some people, but I believe this nails it down pretty quickly as it makes us depend on the work of the Holy Spirit to keep us in line with the plan of God. If not, we will remain out of control to pursue our every fancy.

True self-control or restraint can only be accomplished with the help and power of the Lord. You cannot be the best spiritual person and example without the Lord. And I am sure you have tried to grow in your own strength, just like I have, so I pose this question to you: how did that work long term? Yes, it may have worked for a little while, but without the power of God, it will not last because our strength and will power will eventually run out.

Some translations use the word temperance. In the end, it is self-control or allowing the Spirit of God to guide and direct us in the way of spiritual growth. I am so glad that I do not have to go at this all by myself. I, like you, have often appeared like the myth of Sisyphus attempting to roll the heavy boulder uphill. Sisyphus was delegated by Zeus to do this for life. To make the point, I am glad we have help from the Lord and that He is able to carry and take all our burdens. In many respects, we were not taught to grow daily in our individual discipleship plan. For that matter, were we really discipled? If not, don't worry, God will send people your way if you are honestly seeking to become more like Him.

The next area for excurses is patience. Patience is a tough trait to discuss because it takes patience to develop patience. From firsthand experience, I am here to tell you as a faithful witness that patience is largely developed by going through hardships or trauma. I am shaking my head as I write this because I am recalling the story of Job and how he was tested, tempted, and tried during his ordeal, yet he remained faithful under the pressure of false accusations from friends and horrific attacks on his family, wealth, and mental health from Satan. Job is the poster child for enduring hardships.

Perseverance or patient endurance is a measure of steadfastness that only comes from God's mighty strength and power. You will not be able to hold up in your strength when you are being tested. This will be your personal growth moment. I assure you that you will mature. Sadly, if we do not learn the lessons, we will face the situation over again. I know this brings in the question of suffering. However, this is not my intent, and

I will not be able to unpack the theology of suffering at this point. I only mention the idea as a reference to facilitate spiritual growth and maturity.

As I write this segment, I am approaching this with mixed emotions because we struggle with the idea of "how can a good God allow bad things to happen to good people?" Again, I am not setting out to answer that question in this chapter. In that vein, I am only saying that God will give you the strength and patient endurance to make it through every test and trial. In the end, suffering is redemptive because it draws us closer to God.

The next area for discussion will be less controversial. Godliness is often stated but is less understood. Godliness is a way of life that encompasses on one hand a reverence toward God, and on the other hand devotional worship. Godliness is where we offer true worship to God by a life well lived. Ultimately, God is honored by the ongoing worship or respect we give beyond Sunday. Additional growth will arrive as we learn to love other Christians with a love of the Lord. Brotherly kindness carries a great meaning. The idea is to have a warm, familial feeling toward your Christian brothers and sisters, just like in the first century. Caring for one another or caring for the needs of others is the idea.

The thought is enriched by the notion that we are related to each other in Christ. We are bound by His blood. The idea of tender affection for one another comes to mind; it portrays a family system that has a bond of unity. The test arises because we do not always get along and we want our own way. However, brotherly love makes us grow because we are able to serve others and work together for a greater cause.

Moreover, we are asked to love each other as Christ loved us. *Agape* is the word here, while the former thought was *phileo*, or brotherly love. Agape is a pure love; it is not tainted by the flesh. Agape is the highest form of love or care for someone. This is where the growth takes place because we are told to love each other whether we like them or not. However, I did not write the text. I have to follow it, just like you, if I am going to grow and improve in my spiritual walk.

Finally, we are told that if we possess these qualities, we will never be barren or unfruitful in the knowledge of our Lord Jesus Christ. The interpretation is that if we ascribe to these principles, we will be continual vessels for His growth and glory. The key idea is to be fruitful because unfruitful is not the best option. Being unfruitful carries the unwanted burden of being profitless or useless. God wants the best for us in ministry. He wants us to grow and become fruit bearers for the work or ministry He has for us. Another view of unfruitful is to be filled with thoughts and actions that are not of God. Truly, this is a travesty because God desires for us to be fruitful. In short, we should desire to possess these spiritual characteristics in an effort to grow into a mature being where our actions reflect Him.

04

Desiring God and Denying Self

If anyone desires to come after Me, let him deny himself,
and take up his cross, and follow Me

– MATTHEW 16:24 NKJV

Desire is a major key for spiritual growth—it is more than "want to." I believe it is "have to" or "need to." I say that because we want to do a lot of things. Some of us want to lose weight, while some want to get in shape. As a matter of fact, some have wanted to get in shape or lose weight for a long time. However, have to is more urgent. It carries a greater meaning for the task at hand.

In terms of war, the United States had to get involved in World War II after Hitler invaded Poland on September 1, 1939, with the horrible mission to eradicate the Jewish race. The United States was forced to make a response after Japan bombed Pearl Harbor on December 7, 1941. At this point, we had to get involved on a deeper level. This is the difference that pushed us over the edge to defend our freedoms and to make the world a better place.

As Christians, we are called to make the world a better place by desiring to follow Christ. In Matthew 16:24, Jesus lays out a premise for sacrifice and growth. The declaration is clear—we must first desire to follow and learn. Desire means to possess a strong feeling for or have a passion for something. However, growth is deeper—it will require the power of God to impart the wisdom after we have prayed, studied, and meditated on His word. Growth will require us to work in tandem with God to accomplish this lifelong feat. Desire at the core is where the believer is inspired by God to want more out of a mundane spiritual walk. God begins to take over believers' hearts to make them want more from His presence in them. Jesus says to His disciples that they must desire to follow where He leads them.

Desire, as we know, can be positive or negative. Following Jesus for the right reasons and motives will be a positive experience if we are devoted to growing daily. Yes, there will be setbacks and we will experience ridicule from others with our motives being questioned, but I would not trade this walk for any amount of money, fame, or fortune. I have learned a few things over the years and one of them is simply this: you cannot buy the peace granted by God with physical resources—it can only be given by the Maker, Sustainer, and Creator.

Spiritual growth, like peace, comes from the desire to follow Jesus. He is calling us to follow as He was calling His disciples to follow Him on a continual basis. Following Jesus or growing in our faith requires that we deny the opportunities of the flesh provided by the world. Spiritual maturity and spiritual growth will require a specific denial of the flesh to reach the desired outcomes. Specifically, Jesus mentions that we should deny self. This means we are to follow Him in true discipleship. True discipleship is where we become a student or follower of Christ. The test is following Jesus while denying selfish wants and desires that have the potential to lead us away from true dependance on Jesus.

In a lot of cases, I have witnessed followers, but not faithfulness. By this, I mean that they attend worship, but they are never truly converted. They are afraid to fully surrender, and they follow at a distance because they are fearful that the relationship will cost them more than they are willing to give. Growth happens when we fully surrender and follow Jesus. Surrender is tough because it demands that we respond in obedience to His teachings.

The test is this: are we willing to forsake all to follow and conform to the ways of Jesus? The denying of the flesh is only one aspect as it relates to growth. If possible, let me attempt to stretch you a bit to think deeper about your daily quiet time and growth with God. Jesus is asking us to follow Him because He knows that we need Him as our Sustainer. In fact, when we choose to follow Him, we will begin to be strengthened in ways that we never experienced before. In the case of the disciples, they were enriched by His mere presence, and they witnessed His miracles firsthand. The experience of denying self would draw them closer to Him, to God, and to each other. As Christians, we need this experience with Christ; we need this time daily with Christ to develop. This time was needed by the disciples so they could experience it for themselves. They would watch Him heal the sick and give sight to the blind. Moreover, they were able to see His daily routine for three years. The routine would ground them in prayer, study, and fasting. As disciples, they would see the numerous encounters with people who needed help. He walked with them, and He will walk with us because He is the living God, and He desires that we come after Him out of obedience.

Next, we are told to take up our cross and follow. Sacrifice is eminent within this phrase because Jesus, who is our King and risen Savior, was crucified at Calvary. The cross is no laughing matter—it meant death to Jesus and many of His followers in the early centuries. The cross is a preview of the sacrifices that we must make to develop a deeper appreciation for the horrible acts committed against Him. Spiritual growth will require sacrifice on many levels. We will be asked to let friends walk and let other relationships go who are not headed in the same direction Christ is leading us.

On a deeper note, taking up our cross is dying to ourselves in a spiritual manner that may be uncomfortable now but will yield long-term results. Yes, I know this is hard to comprehend, but trust me, it will be useful. As the old saying goes, "if it were easy, everyone would be doing it." A better example may be the words from the old song by Johnny Cash, "I Walk the Line" (recorded on April 2, 1956, at Sun Studio in Memphis, Tennessee). Jesus is calling us to walk the line toward Him. He is asking us to take up the cross, which is a clear statement of open confession. It is a clear statement that I am no longer walking with the world—I am walking with the higher authority on spiritual matters.

Next, we are asked to follow. Yes, follow. Not lead, but follow. We must remember God is the potter and we are the clay. We are to follow Christ by desiring a deeper relationship, denying self, and taking up our cross; hence, we are to resemble and become more like Him based on His actions. The idea is to closely resemble His ways and the actions He purported. The picture may also include us closely walking by His side to catch every word and deed. Following is a closeness that stems from a desire to know His ways. Following Christ is to truly know His being, inner character, and transformative power. My friends, this is growth, by being in His presence on a daily basis in our quiet time and throughout the day for spiritual consultations. Wow, what a privilege to be close to the greatest person who ever walked the face of the earth! Following Jesus is no easy matter in the beginning, but it gets easier with time because we grow to trust His perfect will for our lives. In summary, growing in Christ is a daily plan that requires individual desire, self-denial, taking up our cross, and following Jesus.

05

Discipleship

Make disciples of all the nations, baptizing them in the name of
the Father and of the Son and of the Holy Spirit

– MATTHEW 28:19 NKJV

Discipleship is where Christians grow in the true image of Christ. Spiritual growth is gained when we allow someone to provide this type of guidance to help us improve our spiritual condition. Notice, I used the term "guide." Good discipleship equals good spiritual guidance. Discipleship is both a process of short-term and long-term growth. The growth occurs when we allow God to work through someone who has greater knowledge and skills. Remember, we are not born full grown in a spiritual sense. Discipleship is a process where new members agree to allow someone to teach them the basic principles of the faith and how to grasp greater spiritual concepts that will improve their lives. It is within this age-old relationship that the believer will become stronger in their walk.

Spiritual maturity and growth will not occur without some type of discipleship. Yes, we can grow through study, reading, and prayer. Discipleship is where the teacher is consistently infusing biblical knowledge and character into another's being. Let me warn you, please be on the alert for individuals who have an oppressive style of discipleship. This approach only makes people harsh and rigid in their thinking toward others. This approach teaches the rules and does not promote a proper relationship with Christ. Hence, discipleship is where we trust God for growth through His Word with the help of an earthly teacher.

Discipleship requires a student-teacher relationship based in Scripture with the idea that the student will mainly learn from the teacher. Also, the teacher may gain a few things from the student. Again, this is not a relationship of control; it is a relationship where the teacher displays genuine love for the pupil in that he wants the student to grow in the knowledge of spiritual things. Discipleship is not a fast process where knowledge is exchanged as commerce like the floor of the New York Stock Exchange. No, discipleship is a slower process where a teacher shares the impregnated Word of God with a willing student who is hungry for growth and development. Discipleship is a slower Crock-Pot method of preparing and cooking a meal that creates great flavors within the dish once prepared. In one way, we are being prepared for ministry to be "the salt of the earth" (Matthew 5:13).

Spiritual growth is related to discipleship through the fact that we all need the right environment to grow and flourish for the Kingdom. Discipleship, if done properly, will assist believers young and old in this manner. The term "discipleship" also means follower. We are ultimately following Christ. We are ultimately living in the teachings of Christ. As Paul said, "Imitate me, just as I also imitate Christ" (1 Corinthians 11:1-2 NKJV). This is the real test. Are we following Christ? Discipleship will work to create a deeper intimacy with God. This intimacy will pay dividends in the long run because every Christian will be challenged in their faith at some point.

Discipleship is where the student grows toward God. Yes, the basic tenets should be taught in an effort to ground and connect individuals to a greater, more meaningful relationship to Christ. Good discipleship expands the relationship with Christ. Discipleship that promotes any other program will prove to be ineffective in the long run because the focus is not Christ-centric.

Spiritual growth through discipleship can be one-on-one or within a larger community. Christians need community, they always have and always will. The Christians in the first century had a deep love for Christ and one another. The community helped them through hard times. The community banded together when they were oppressed by the Roman government. Discipleship in concept is where we become students led by a God-fearing teacher. In Scripture, we see Jesus calling His disciples in Matthew 4:18-22. We further see this played out as Paul guided Timothy in 1 Timothy 1:2. The Bible also notes the relationship of Elijah and Elisha in 1 Kings 19:19. Discipleship promotes growth by reading, studying, and doing. The student in the biblical days would spend extensive amounts of time with their rabbi. The rabbi played a key role in their spiritual development. Jesus was the disciples' rabbi, and they would follow Him for three years as He healed the sick and provided for the needs of the spiritual community. Speaking of rabbi, the rabbi would serve as a spiritual father to the student for the sake of growth and development.

Next in good spiritual discipleship is the idea of multiplication. The disciple, if trained and nurtured properly, would be able to help and share the gospel with others. Discipleship is multiplication, which is growth and growing the Kingdom. Discipleship may be the forgotten engagement of this generation in that so many Christians are so deep into the Internet that we have forgotten to be connected to people so we can help them grow. In short, I think the church moving forward will need to be "high tech and high touch" with members in general and with discipleship. If possible, I will try to explain. Members need community to grow and thrive. The communities can be online and in person. Moreover, for members to stay and mature into healthy Christians, good discipleship must take place. As members grow in community, they are able to meet other like-minded individuals with whom they will develop bonds that foster fellowship and Christian connections. Life groups are a great way for members to be discipled and connected to one another and to Christ. Churches can have both life groups and classes. In general, life groups are about transformation and classes are about information; however, there is a way to do both to promote member growth. The goal of discipleship is growth for the spiritual reason of being useful to the Kingdom and to Christ.

06

Growth through Prayer

Men always ought to pray and not lose heart

– LUKE 18:1 NKJV

Prayer is a powerful source of strength for believers. The story is told about James, the half-brother of Jesus and the writer of the book of James. James was known for his strong prayer life. He was given a nickname that would reflect his devotion to God because he prayed so much. James would be called "Old Camel Knees." The imagery and meaning for the name are powerful. "Old Camel Knees" says it all. James was devoted to God in prayer. The name refers to the way a camel bows before his master in order for the master to place a load on his back. It also refers to the way a camel has callused knees because he bows down to let passengers ride. James was given this name out of respect for his prayer life.

As Christians, we may need to increase our prayer time with God to have an increased awareness of His presence. Prayer is critical to the growth of a believer because it allows two-way communication with God. Communication involves talking and listening. God will respond in a non-audible manner through the Holy Spirit to inform you about His plans or His answer. The answer will not contradict the perfect will of God. The answer will also coincide with the written Word of God because the Word has instructions for living. Prayer for the believer entails making requests to God because we know He can deliver.

However, growth occurs when we are called to remain faithful when we do not receive the answer we are requesting. Growth occurs because we show our dependance on God when we share our concerns with Him in prayer. Dependance is what God wants from each of His created beings. Prayer is that avenue where we are called to rely on God for strength and support.

Prayer is noted as being a part of the spiritual disciplines, along with study, meditation, fasting, submitting, worship, and surrender. The spiritual disciplines are kept as a way to build a better foundation for growth. The spiritual disciplines are in place to move the Christian toward Spiritual Formation, which in the end leads to becoming more Christlike. The goal is to grow daily by becoming more like Christ. Prayer opens the avenue to hear from God.

In general, the babe in Christ has a focus to talk with God without valuing the critical component of listening. Listening to God in prayer is a sign of growth and maturity because this is where we trust God to provide the valuable information needed. We grow by taking our problems and challenges to the Master to get His input for our situation. Growth also occurs because prayer is communion with God. Communion is the deepest fellowship we can desire to have with our Creator. Prayer provides us with this extreme fellowship to draw closer to the mind of God. Prayer is fellowship because we enter the throne room of His presence with the idea that we will be rewarded with help and hope. Prayer is where we draw near to God (James 4:7-8).

Honestly, most Christians do not consistently enjoy this deep interaction on a regular basis because they have a limited or nonexistent prayer life. Prayer is not only growth; it is a recognition that you need God and all the powers of heaven to build a wall of protection against spiritual warfare. Growth happens because we realize that we are unable to fight against Satan by ourselves. Prayer is that spiritual hang-out space where we reflect on the goodness of God because of who He is. Talking to God as though He is a friend is essentially where we develop a devotion to God. This devotion carries us through the day. In one respect, we should pray our way through the day as the Scriptures state in 1 Thessalonians 5:17. Consistent devotion aids the believer with guidance from the Holy Spirit.

With that said, I firmly believe that Christians should spend quiet time with God each day as a measure of obedience and fellowship. The Bible speaks of drawing near to God in James 4:8. Prayer may also be considered as worship because we bow before God in adoration for His goodness. The key idea is to come consistently before God with reverence, humility, and thanksgiving. Growth continues to occur because we thank Him for His numerous blessings and grace. Maturity is displayed because we are showing appreciation for the things that God has worked out for us.

In many cases, we are too busy to pray. This shows that spiritual things may not be the priority we thought they were. Sometimes we get tired of waiting on God in prayer and we begin to doubt and fret. God hears our every cry and stands ready to deliver on our requests. In all honesty, I had to grow to accept His answers. Yes, this is a sign of maturity if you can accept His will.

God has three or four main answers, and they center around yes, no, and not right now. I have also seen a maybe in some cases. Yes is when Hezekiah was sick and prayed and was granted fifteen more years to live (2 Kings 20:1-6). No is found when Paul prayed three times for God to remove the thorn and God responded with the classic statement in 2 Corinthians 12:9, "My grace is sufficient." God will also tell us to wait or will remain silent as we continue to approach Him as revealed with Hannah in 1 Samuel 1:20. Hannah was under deep duress as she went and prayed on a yearly basis at the commanded time for a son. The text reads "in the process of time" (GNV). God can move, but He sometimes makes us wait to work us through the process. Furthermore, I believe God may put conditions on situations that may be okay for us. The conditions center around seeing if we will remain faithful. In summary, spiritual growth is going to God in prayer with our every need.

07

Growth through Continuous Study

Study to show yourself approved

– 2 TIMOTHY 2:15 MEV

Bible study will cause growth if we study with an open heart and mind. God expects the Christian to study to gain knowledge of the sacred text as well as of His divine nature. However, growth may be limited when we only study issues of doctrine. Let me be clear, doctrine is important, and it has its place to help Christians form into stronger individuals. However, a continual inpouring of basic doctrine about baptism, salvation, repentance, communion, and giving often leads to Christian immaturity. Again, I am not against the basics of the faith or teaching foundational matters of Scripture. I am thinking of Hebrews 6:1, where the writer stresses that believers should move past the elementary tenets of the faith and move to completeness. In many cases, church members are trapped at an early stage of discipleship. In the end, if changes are not made, they will only stay at the beginning stages, never maturing into individuals that can be used by God in mighty ways.

The context of this passage starts in the later verses of chapter 5 where the statement is contrasted between requiring milk or solid food. The idea as it relates to growth is clear—mature or growing Christians are able to digest or process the Bible on a different level. However, in contrast, younger individuals in the faith, no matter their age, will only be able to accept milk. The passage in Hebrews 5:13 calls them babes. Further, the same verse says they are "unskilled in the word."

So, back to studying and answering how we experience growth through the Word, we are challenged to move toward perfection or completeness in Hebrews 6:1. As you can see, the passage is one complete thought from Hebrews 5:12 – 6:3. The Hebrew writer is asking us to grow a more complete faith. In one sense, we are asked to stretch. The word used is "perfection," which carries the idea of completeness. As Christians, we should be working to become complete individuals with the help of Christ. The word perfection or completion also covers the idea of working through the stages of spiritual growth. In the case of growth through study, the above passage takes into consideration the notion that we should be building on the basic foundation as we move further in our spiritual walk.

Studying the Bible requires that we have comprehension of the basics that set the stage for growth. The idea is to grow while building on what you have learned previously. Studying will mean to investigate for revealed truth. Investigating the Word of God will keep you sharp and searching for greater discoveries.

Later in this chapter, we will provide a few suggestions to enrich your study time. However, for now, we will attempt to capture the connection for studying and growth. In fact, studying is listed among the spiritual disciplines of prayer, reading, meditation, fasting, worship, service, and surrender. The reasons for study are numerous and will not be exhausted in this frame. However, your individual approach to studying will make a difference as you grow in your faith.

Studying should begin with prayer as a means to open our hearts to God for His reveal. In many instances, we open our Bibles, cell phones, or tablets without consulting God for divine guidance as we seek to know more. This approach often leads to limited discovery and growth. Praying for God to reveal His truth is also a measure of humility because we are asking God for help to grow and to consider additional areas where we may be deficient, or we approach God with our traditions, and we are never able to receive greater transformation from His living Word. Study is growth and will be fun as you discover concepts that would have otherwise remained unseen to the untrained eye. In addition, you will be frustrated as you yearn to know more, but the Holy Spirit will only reveal greater knowledge when you are ready to rightly divide His redeeming Word.

Studying for growth will also take time and tools. I promise you that to really grow, you will need to spend extensive time pouring through commentaries, Bible dictionaries, and the Bible itself. All in all, remember the ultimate goal is to become more Christlike or complete in His image. As a reminder, the sole priority of study is not knowledge for the sake of quoting the Bible or parading our faith in the face of others as a way to say, "Look at me, I am smart." Ultimately, studying should draw you into a deeper relationship with God, the Father, and the Son.

Knowledge is powerful and is needed to defend the faith against false teachers. However, knowledge of God should result in a greater faith. It should manifest into a transformed and redeemed life. Moreover, wisdom is primo, like a fine wine that has aged and become of greater value over time. A quick tangent: I know some legalist is coming unglued right now about my wine analogy. For the record, I am not a drinker. I only use that analogy to make a point about studying because we should get better with time. Furthermore, any true Bible student will know that the Bible does not condemn drinking—it prohibits drunkenness. Okay, before your blood pressure is elevated and you seek to cancel me, please read Galatians 5:21. As a matter of fact, please read it in numerous translations and please read for context and clarity.

Next, I will spend time discussing the benefits of reading the Bible on a daily basis. Reading is also listed as a spiritual discipline. Reading helps the Christian discover the true nature of God. Studying is not to be confused with reading, although you must read to study. Reading, like studying, is absolutely necessary for growth and maturity. As a matter of fact, we should read Scripture each day as we carve out quiet time with God. This quiet time is valuable as we pray and seek direction for the day. Reading is essential for growth because it, like studying, takes time. God is always pleased when we lay aside time to learn and understand Him on a deeper level. Reading on a daily basis is not just an exercise, it is a discipline where we form a habit to seek to understand God more fully. Bible reading is devotion to God because we are seeking to be connected to the mind and heart of God.

Okay, back to studying. I will attempt within this final section to give you a few suggestions to make your study time more beneficial. As stated before, I suggest that you start with prayer. Prayer opens your heart to God and what He wants you to grasp. I also suggest that you get a good study Bible or download a good app on your phone that has additional notes, word studies, and background information about the book and particular Scripture that you are studying,

Next, I would begin by reading the passage five or six times as a way to gain a greater understanding of the plain meaning of the text. Officially, this is a modified version of a process called *Lectio Divina*, or divine reading. Divine reading allows the text to speak directly to you with less distortion from human sources. Studying after praying and reading the text multiple times should involve understanding the immediate context, the broader context, the historical context, and the sociocultural background.

Context should also include who wrote it, when it was written, where it was written, and why it was written. Knowledge of these areas will help the student in their exegesis.

Please keep in mind, context is king. By this, I mean context is of critical importance. Exegesis is to draw or pull background information from the text. Exegesis encompasses historical settings and grammatical aspects of the text. Furthermore, you might ask if there are any grammatical issues with the text based on scribal or copying errors.

Next, a good Bible student will seek to follow a few good hermeneutical rules. Hermeneutics is the science of biblical interpretation. Interpretation is important because you first want to discover what the text meant to them in the biblical days. This is an important step to understand and explore. In other words, how would they have heard the narrative? How would they have heard the story or parable? What did it mean to them in their day and culture? Establishing the first meaning of the text must be done before we attempt to apply a modern-day application. By this, I am suggesting that you put on a set of first century glasses and read the text from that perspective. My friends, this is a good Bible study practice.

Next, a good Bible interpretation for the layman or scholar should include knowing the type of information you are reading because you will view the books of poetry differently from epistles, parables, and gospels. All in all, you are seeking information with key terms and context before you determine application.

08

Fasting – The Forgotten Task

When you fast, do not be like the hypocrites

– MATTHEW 6:16 NKJV

Fasting is the next area for discussion. I must admit, fasting is not my favorite spiritual pastime. Fasting requires discipline and communion with God. Fasting is where we decide to give up something or place something on temporary hold so we might obtain something greater from God.

The process of fasting has always been frightful for me. Yes, I have fasted on numerous occasions for as long as seven days and as short as one. Please, do not take that as bragging because I have fasted for seven days with only water or juice—I needed it. It changed me. Honestly, I need to fast at least once a week for a few hours once I wake until lunch. I have learned that God will provide. He will give me strength.

I remember the entire church fasting in Topeka, Kansas. Wow, we made it through. As I think back, it was a great time of spiritual deliverance and healing of the mind. We fasted for spiritual direction and strength. We fasted for discernment and deliverance from sin. We fasted to gain a deeper knowledge. Let me be completely honest, I was worried because I had a busy schedule then, and I wondered how I was going to make it seven days without food and only having water. It was rough at first with the headaches and the doubt. But God grew me up, once I began to trust Him more and more. I only tell the story to be transparent and to let you know that even now when I fast, I generally hit a rough space mentally for a short time until I fully turn it over to God.

Fasting is only one vehicle by which we gain strength from God. Fasting will also help you gain spiritual insights to your deepest self. The process of fasting is where we decide to give up something for a period in an effort to draw closer to God. During this time of abstinence, we should be spending excessive amounts of time in prayer. Prayer is key when fasting because you are able to talk to God on a different level than normal. Prayer while fasting allows you to hear from God in ways like never before because you are stripped bare before Him, like someone who has nothing. In these moments, we are vulnerable before God and in the deepest need for His care and strength. Fasting is where we as Christians show true dependance on Him for strength and deliverance.

I recall the days back at my previous church when we met every evening at six thirty to pray for each other in a show of strength and community. We were able to encourage one another to believe in the faithfulness of God. I suggest that you fast as a church community for the right cause. I suggest that you fast as men in your life groups or classes because it will help you overcome your struggles. I offer that all ministry leaders fast to gain a better clarity for ministry direction. I implore you to fast for others who are struggling with addictions, for wayward spouses, and for crazy teenagers. Fasting should never be routine or for the sake of doing it to get attention. Fasting is so real that we meet God, and we are able to gain a deeper appreciation for His love and care.

For the sake of clarity, fasting is not a New Testament command—it is optional because we turn everything over to Him out of obedience rather than obligation. Generally speaking, fasting is a private matter between you and God (Matthew 6:18). I only mention what we did as a church with hopes that it would encourage you to consider it as an option. Fasting is the real test of denying the flesh because you will want what you have decided to forfeit.

Fasting can be accomplished in many ways without giving up food—it can include giving up TV, social media, Facebook, TikTok, or soap operas. The point is to temporarily give up something that you love, need, or want for the sole purpose of gaining a deeper time of communion with God. Fasting can be for one, two, or three days, or even more. Fasting does not always mean giving up food for the entire time. Fasting can be giving up coffee or sodas. Fasting can be giving up bread or carbohydrates. Again, there are many ways to accomplish the task.

Caution, if you have medical conditions, please check with your physician before you attempt fasting for any length of time. Abstaining from food for those with certain medical conditions may not be the best way to participate in fasting. You may be better suited to give up coffee, sweets, TV, social media, radio, cussing, arguing, or complaining. The principle is still the same, you decide to deny yourself of something that you want or think you need. Fasting is ultimately refusing the flesh to obtain a greater spiritual fellowship with God. Fasting should always be accompanied with prayer because prayer is where we gain strength in our times of weakness (Romans 8:26).

In summary, you will grow if you choose to fast. However, with fasting, your motives must be pure. Fasting has a way of exposing you when you are not being honest with God. In addition, I suggest that you have a strong spiritual walk because fasting is not for the faint of heart. Finally, I suggest that you break your fast slowly if you have gone without food for a few days. Slowly breaking your fast and returning to small amounts of food will allow your system to readjust within a natural rhythm.

09

Full Surrender

Take up his cross daily, and follow Me

– LUKE 9:23 NKJV

Surrender is a tough biblical thought to fully process because it requires so much self-sacrifice and obedience. Surrender is a call for a dynamic change in your spiritual journey. Surrender was asked of every major and minor biblical character because without surrender, we would follow our own self-centered devices.

Jesus tells His followers to deny themselves in the above passage. Surrender is where we critically examine our thinking and ask ourselves, "Am I living the best life I can for Christ?" The Christian is tasked with the idea to self-surrender because we have free will. God gave us free will. Free will gives us the ability to make choices—good, bad, or indifferent. However, surrendering to God moves us one step closer to finding the best that God may have hidden for us in this maze we call life.

Full surrender requires that we allow God to order our steps (Psalms 37:23). The Lord will guide each of the steps we take if we would only give into the plans that He has for us. Surrender is going all in for the Master and there is no way to lessen our responsibility. Spiritual growth demands surrender. Surrender is hard because we have relied so much on our own fleshly ways and thinking. We have made null the enlightenment of Proverbs 3:5-7, where it is written that we should trust in the Lord with all our heart while refusing to lean to our own understanding.

Next, we must tackle the tough subject of death. Death is not a popular subject, but surrender is death. It requires that we die to self as a passage to a better life that is more fulfilled with Christ. Surrender is death at the deepest level. This concept smacks us in the face because it is brutal and raw. Yes, full surrender is dying to the old person and habits that will hang around if we do not die to the natural man that seeks resurrection. Oftentimes, we keep the old person on life support because we are fearful that we cannot make it without him or her. Death in this case enables us to live freely in Christ Jesus.

In truth, we must learn to think differently and live life fully for Christ. Surrender is not just Christ speak or good church talk. Surrender requires actions that will lead us to better mental and physical spaces. Surrender is also a military term that means we give in and follow instructions from superiors if we want to live. With that imagery, we surrender by turning ourselves in so that we might be liberated at a later time. Surrender has a mandate that requires that we follow the example of Jesus when He fully gave into His Father's will as He made the choice to go to the cross of calvary for our sins. Full surrender leaves no room to turn back to our old ways because we realize that we are so much better as new creations in Christ.

For many, full surrender is a mammoth proposition. The proposition feels unattainable. You are correct, full surrender is unattainable in your own strength. You must rely and depend on God. Full surrender is best described as Saul of Tarsus being converted to Christianity on the road to Damascus in Acts 9. Saul was persecuting the church. He was working against the promises of God. God stepped in as Saul was on a road trip to harm more believers. God said enough and struck him with blindness. God would send Ananias to assist Paul in his conversion. The text says that scales fell from his eyes. Paul had to surrender. The Lord asked him, "Why are you kicking against me?" (Acts 9:5). Paul would respond, "Who are You, Lord?" and "What do You want me to do?" (Acts 9:5-6).

Honestly, there is some Paul in all of us. We were fighting for the wrong team or serving the wrong master. We needed redirecting. We had to surrender, and God would walk with us each day to become better. Moreover, lack of surrender creates problems from the perspective of obedience. Surrender is just that and more. Jonah refused to surrender to God, and this caused him to be thrown overboard at sea and to be swallowed by a big fish. This experience caused a change in his attitude. He finally surrendered and went to his original required destination.

Total surrender is displayed when we change our actions to reflect those of Christ. The action of surrender is where we fully disown our past nature to follow in the footsteps of Jesus. Yes, we are to disown the nature that makes us work against the transformed nature that God expects. Surrender is dying numerous deaths each day to wholly please Christ. In one respect, it is the constant rendering of our lives to be managed and maintained by the Holy Spirit.

As humans, we are taught never to surrender because it shows weakness, especially in sports. If possible, let me give an example and I hope I will not be sued. I know of a professional football team in the South. They are an okay team from year to year. In fact, they have not won a Super Bowl in quite a while. You know the team—they have a powerful owner who manages a lot of the day-to-day operations. The team has a big fan base. Some say that the team would be better if the owner would turn the operations over to others in the front office who better understand players of this generation and the NFL of today. The point they are making is that if the team remains structured the way it is now, it will not win a Super Bowl in the near future because it has too much interference from the owner. Yes, he can do what he wishes because he is the owner, and he has power and money. However, unless he surrenders the team to the front office personnel, general manager, and coaches, the team will continue to be okay and make great amounts of money at the box office, but they will not win a Super Bowl until change happens.

We are the same way as Christians—until we surrender our daily actions to the One who can fix the problems, we will continue to struggle. This is surrender at its highest peak. It requires that we make space for God by moving things out of the way that hinder a clear vision of the critical objective. Surrender is dying to the desires of the flesh on a daily basis.

10

Putting God First

*Seek first the kingdom of God and His
righteousness*

– MATTHEW 6:33 NKJV

Spiritual growth must be intentional—it is where we make the
things of God a priority. Stephen Covey, in his 1989 book
The 7 Habits of Highly Effective People, wrote a chapter on putting
first things first. The slogan is true in the spiritual world also: we
must develop a plan to put first things first.

In Matthew 6:33, we are encouraged to place spiritual things
at the top of our daily list of activities. These words ring so true—
God must be a priority if we are to grow a personal appreciation
for His goodness and grace. Jesus mentions this Scripture while
teaching the Sermon on the Mount. This sermon mentions
prayer, forgiveness, fasting, money, and worry. Jesus is imploring
us to make spiritual things a superior priority. The right priorities

will be a key factor in your growth and maturity. In so many cases, we are what Augustine railed against when he said that we have "disordered loves."

Again, the things we choose to focus on will determine whether we will be successful on this spiritual journey. Jesus is encouraging Christians to have the right spiritual focus and priorities. The right priorities can serve as blinders to keep us from straying from the path. The first word in the passages invites us to seek or search for the things of righteousness. Seek can also lend itself to desiring what is true. I believe that we should desire to improve our spiritual walk with God. Desire deals with the personal want to improve. However, desire by itself is not good enough. It will take action to bring better results. It will take consistent actions over a long period to really lock in on what God desires from us.

Growth also requires patience as we work things out with God's help as we seek improved realities. Desire goes further to include a firm resolution for improving. Again, the passage encourages us to seek God (Psalms 42:1). However, on another note, I would offer that God has always sought an individual relationship with us (John 6:44). In my view, He has always reached in our direction as a measure of His unending love.

The verse also includes the proclamation that all things above will be granted if we place His Kingdom first. Placing God first is growth within itself because we choose to make the things He requires a priority. Good priorities make it possible for us to remain faithful to God. In Matthew 6:32, the Bible says that God knows what we need. The Scripture makes this claim because God wants us to focus on spiritual things compared to worldly desires. Spiritual priorities require that we set our minds "on things above" (Colossians 3:2). The idea of making God a priority is embedded in Scripture as a way to keep us connected to God.

In addition, seeking God and making Him first is worship. Yes, worship. Worship means to honor and reverence God with our daily actions. Some Christians have limited worship for Sundays only. This may be your corporate practice or official worship day. However, God wants us to worship him every day with our actions. Seeking God is to come before Him with thanksgiving. It is when we put God first that we honor Him with our entire being. Remember, we are to make our priorities revolve around God.

Next, when we do not allow God to take His rightful place, we may, in a borderline way, be creating idols by replacing God with other things. God is not pleased when we do this. In fact, we are growing in the wrong direction. Idols replace God. Idols are a real test of our true spiritual priorities. If we are not careful, we will replace God accidentally. However, some of us replace God on purpose. Again, God wants us to make Him a priority. This pleases Him when we seek to serve and honor Him in our everyday routine.

In summary, we are to place God in His rightful place. The rightful place is at the forefront of our lives. This pleases God and prevents other things from becoming a priority.

11

One More Test – Love Your Enemies

Love your enemies, do good to those who hate you, bless those who curse you, and pray for those who spitefully use you

– LUKE 6:27-28 NKJV

Spiritual growth requires going further than you have gone before with people at your church or spiritual community. Jesus makes a bold statement when He tells us to love our enemies. As the younger generation would say, really? Yes, we must love our enemies. This is where both spiritual growth and maturity come into play because it takes great strength to love your enemies. It is not natural, and for sure, it is not normal.

Jesus is making a stark point with this admonition. Again, He tells us to love our enemies. How does this work? What does this look like? How is this even possible? I will tell you; it is only through a growing and mature relationship with Christ that this is possible. Furthermore, we are not able to accomplish this feat on our own strength. We will need to rely on Christ for this to happen. The idea follows the beatitudes. It is character development. Better yet, it is spiritual character development.

Wow, what a charge! Loving your enemy is a test to see if you will follow Jesus in obedience. Spiritual strength is not developed in the arena of hate. It is when we follow the example of Jesus that we are able to see the greater purpose for the love we possess. In fact, it is His love that dwells within us that we are able to give away as a sign of maturity. The situation requires that we treat them in a respectable manner while being at odds with them. Who knows, the love you show may eventually convict them and cause a change.

Now, I know what you may be thinking—its next to impossible. God is saying love them with the love of the Lord. Obviously, some infraction has occurred, and it is easy not to forgive. With that said, Jesus is calling us to a higher standard. He is asking us to be spirit-filled followers of His church. Yes, I realize that this is not a natural response based on the circumstances. Indeed, this is the proper answer compared to the world. In this way, we are showing both growth and maturity.

Church people will test you. Satan will test you in this area. He wants you to carry a grudge so that he may rob you of your spiritual peace. I wonder how many of us are failing this love test right now. Honestly, I am convicted, and I am writing this book. I am reviewing a few situations in my mind right now that I need to try to rectify. Jesus is calling us to elevate our spiritual personhood through His divine assistance. Again, you will not be able to accomplish the key tenets required in this passage based on your own strength. He is promoting a deeper discovery of spiritual values.

Next, he doubles down to use a blackjack term. Okay, please don't attempt to revoke my Christian hall pass for grace because I used an example from the world. I have learned that if we are going to reach the unsaved or reunite those who have left the faith, we are going to have to meet people where they are and then pour into them with the hope and prayer that they will see the need to reconnect with Christ. People are looking for authenticity and transparency. They are seeking a religion that is useful right now today. Especially men—we claim we want them to participate in our fellowships. To do this, we need real talk and communication on levels they comprehend. Okay, sorry for that tangent, but you get the point. Loving your enemies is a hard ask because it goes against what we have been taught.

Next, we are to do good to those who hate us. Wait a minute, do good to those who hate us? Yes, that's what Jesus said. In scope, this is a choice that we will need to make on our way to maturity. Jesus mentions this because His Kingdom is different. It may not be easy now, but it gets easier to live out because we trust Him for strength. The text asks us to move with compassion where possible. It pulls in the verse where we are told to live at peace with all men "as much as depends on you" (Romans 12:18 NKJV). Again, spiritual maturity demands that we act and think on different levels to see how God can be glorified in each situation. The verse calls us to act like Jesus while He was being persecuted because He did not sin. Hate is a strong word—it is where we detest something or someone. In this case, they hate us. Consequently, you may not hate them, they may hate you. Growth occurs when you are able to rectify this situation.

Next, Jesus adds more to the list. He tells us to bless those who curse us. The idea is to remain steady in your walk while enduring these situations. The point of the section is not to strike back in anger or react like them. Remember, we are called to a higher standard. This is the spiritual maturity we are asked to display. Also, we should be in control of our actions. Of course, this displays spiritual growth and maturity.

In addition, we are asked to pray for those who knowingly use us. I wish the demand became easier, but it doesn't. We are called to respond in a Christlike manner—this is the spiritual maturity that is required for continued growth. The next may be the toughest of all requests in the manner of turning the other cheek in Luke 6:29. Although it is tough, it was made easy by Jesus as He endured the horrors of the cross. Carefully, we are to follow the example of Jesus. It will be hard at times because we live in this sinful world, and we will be tempted to redeem or justify our actions. However, let us remember that the example has already been set and we should follow it in order to foster spiritual growth and maturity.

12

Things That Hinder Growth

My little children, these things I write to you, so that
you may not sin

– 1 JOHN 2:1 NKJV

S in in general will prevent spiritual growth and maturity. Sin is the process or action of missing the mark. Yes, I included the word "process" in the previous sentence because I believe we can fall through a series of events designed by Satan to defeat and destroy our testimony. In James 1:14, it mentions that we are "drawn away" by our "own desires and enticed." This sounds like a process that is sent from the devil to lead Christians astray.

Sin in all forms will hinder spiritual growth. The ultimate goal is for us to deny the flesh, which means making a commitment to trust God for deliverance. John the Apostle declares in 1 John 2:1 that we should not sin. However, if we sin we have an Advocate to redeem us. Let's be clear, we "all have sinned and come short of the glory of God" (Romans 3:23 NJV). However, sin serves to separate us from the blessings provided by God (Isaiah 59:1-2). With that said, we are striving to get better in our walk so that we do not sin by omission or commission. Honestly, everyone has at least one struggle if they are being transparent. As noted earlier, sin can and will hinder spiritual growth because we give into a situation, and it has the potential to pull us in directions that will draw us away from God.

Next, we will cover additional sins that have the potential to hinder spiritual growth as seen in Galatians 5:19-21 (NKJV). The list includes "adultery, fornication, uncleanness, lewdness, idolatry, sorcery, hatred, contentions, jealousies, outbursts of wrath, selfish ambitions, dissensions, heresies, envy, murders, drunkenness, revelries, and the like." This list of sins covers the gamut and makes it clear that these items work against growth and development. For the sake of this project, we will only list the sins in Galatians without fully unpacking each one individually. Galatians 5:21 sends a stern warning not to practice sin because the results can be dire. In addition, we are told in Galatians 5:16 to "walk in the Spirit" as a way to defeat the flesh. Remember, Satan knows and understands each weakness that we have, and he is sure to exploit them if we do not seek to grow away from these tendencies.

On another note, arrogance or pride can wreak havoc in our lives. Pride comes before the fall (Proverbs 16:18). In addition, "the lust of the flesh, the lust of the eyes, and the pride of life" found in 1 John 2:15-16 (NKJV) can serve to stifle our spiritual growth. In numerous cases, sin is overlooked through the process of perfect rationalization. Sin stifles the relationship with God because we serve our selfish nature. This selfish nature is only conquered when we fully surrender and allow God to lead. We must get honest with ourselves and avoid certain people, places, or things that can cause us to stray from the path.

Paul, in Romans 13:14 (NKJV), makes a note to tell us that we should "make no provision for the flesh." In one way, we should not allow the flesh any room to spawn into tempting situations. The flesh is the leader when it comes to making excuses to sin. Growth occurs as we fight each day to defeat Satan with the help of the Holy Spirit.

As one more reminder, sin lurks at the door (Genesis 4:7) to draw us away from the safety of grace. However, to defeat sin on a consistent basis we will need to rely more on the Word of God as Jesus did in Matthew 4 when He was tempted by Satan. Moreover, we will need to put on the whole armor of God (Ephesians 6:10-17). In addition, we might want to develop a battle plan that includes prayer, study, accountability, and resistance techniques. In the end, we should be working to defeat sin so that we can experience spiritual growth and maturity. Please note, there are other sins that may not be listed here. With that said, please work to overcome your own personal sins by trusting God for deliverance.

13

Discernment

There is a way that seems right to a man, but its end is the way of death

– PROVERBS 14:12 NKJV

Spiritual maturity includes discernment. Discernment in spiritual matters means that you are able to process information and make the best choices in view of Scripture. Discernment in many respects is a gift from God because you are able to see spiritual things in a broader manner. In fact, discernment is seeing things as God would see them. Immaturity works against the call of God on your life. It holds you back from seeing the best God has to offer. Spiritual immaturity will not let you see the greater ministry that God is shaping for your life. Discernment is trusting that God knows best for your life. Discernment shows spiritual maturity because this is where we put into practice the things that we know to be true based on Scripture.

To discern a situation means to decide the best option that pleases God. Furthermore, discernment is an act of judging between multiple variables that may look equal without any differences. However, we must remember the statement in Proverbs 16:25 where it states, "There is a way that seems right to a man, but its end is the way of death." Spiritual discernment captures the notion that we must pass judgment on a choice to make the right determination of what to do next. Discernment is a state of mind where we pass sentence on something as a way to ferret out the best choice.

Proper discernment was not used by Jonah in the beginning as he decided to work against God and go to Tarshish after being told by God to travel to Nineveh. Spiritual decisions lay at the core of discernment. Jonah decided to do what he wanted to do in spite of clear directions from God. Jonah personally signed himself up for unnecessary heartache and pain.

Do you see it, when we go against the will of God, we officially sign ourselves up for things that can cause hurt and pain. Let's face it, we have enough struggles in general, so why add to the issues you are already facing? Moreover, we must realize that Satan is plotting as we speak to send hurt, harm, harassment, and other horrendous acts your way. Let me be clear, I believe the horrors and hurts we face are directed by Satan and not God. But as it relates to discernment, this is tough to accept in our minds. However, discernment helps us through this process because we have grown to trust God entirely. Discernment also helps us to manage events better because we know that God would never intentionally hurt His people. God allows things to fall our way because man sinned in the garden.

Discernment helps us understand the fact that we all have free will to make decisions that comply or compete with God's will. The Bible is replete with characters that made good and bad decisions. We often mention David and his encounter with Bathsheba. David had a choice in this matter, but he was led by the flesh. Yes, the flesh is a hard thing to manage because it deals with desire. In terms of discernment, David made a mess of his life in this situation. Spiritual discernment would have changed the outcome in this situation because he would have made a different decision in this matter. Yet, he followed his natural thinking, and it had consequences.

Discernment could also be called spiritual decision-making. Spiritual decision-making for people of faith should be shaped around a metric that calculates possible outcomes. The process should include a series of questions that provoke cognitive awareness before the actions are taken. In fact, one bad action has the potential to produce other actions of the same consequence. The list of questions for spiritual discernment may help as you make decisions:

What are my true motives?
Why do I really want this?
Will this opportunity or situation pull me away from or draw me closer to God?
If I get this, what will I become?

Since I have had this relationship or new opportunity, do I have increased peace or additional misery?

These questions will assist with discernment. In consequence, they will help assist the believer in making major decisions. Good decisions are the basis for a life that honors God. The believer is generally tasked with the challenge of making decisions that coincide with the will of God. The above questions are listed as a guide and may not be all inclusive. However, hopefully they will be beneficial to readers as they ponder decisions that impact their future. The questions will provide a way to measure the pure and impure motives that are in play when we are making critical decisions. Critical decisions are common as we consider the choices we are exploring to be in tune with God's will.

Spiritual discernment is only one sign of maturity. In Proverbs 4:7, Solomon extols us to get an understanding when gaining wisdom. Earlier, I offered a negative example of Jonah from the sacred text. Now, I would like to use a more favorable example of a Bible character who made the right decision while under pressure. Yes, spiritual maturity will require Christ-followers to make the right spiritual decisions while experiencing pressure to recall things we know to be true.

With that said, I offer a brief synopsis of Daniel as an example of someone who was able to let their true inner spiritual character shine while they were under extreme pressure to conform to the norms of society. As the narrative goes, Daniel was taken captive by King Nebuchadnezzar. The king was conned into creating a worship decree that prevented anyone from worshiping any god beyond the god of the Medes and the Persians. Daniel had served the king faithfully. In fact, Daniel possessed an "excellent spirit" as told in Daniel 6:3. Daniel had also distinguished himself from the influences of Babylonian captivity. This is where discernment under pressure comes in. The king stamped a decree that made the worship that Daniel offered to the God of Israel invalid. This decree would cause issues for Daniel because he prayed three times a day. The king had no choice but to follow through on the edict, which would place Daniel in the lions' den as punishment for following what he knew was right by serving Yahweh. The die was cast, and Daniel was sent to the lions' den. The king was so shaken that he stayed up all night fasting over the situation. But in the morning, he went to check on Daniel and he called his name and Daniel answered. The king was joyful at the statement of Daniel when he said, "O king, live forever! My God sent His angel and shut the lions' mouths, so that they have not hurt me, because I was found innocent before Him" (Daniel 6:22 NKJV). This is a powerful statement. Daniel stayed true to his integrity and to His God. He was under pressure, but he waited on God and God delivered.

The test of discernment is to remain faithful in our decision-making when we are facing systems, people, and power structures. Finally, God is faithful and will always provide us a way of escape from the unfair situation we are facing.

14

Suffering That Produces Growth and Maturity

Knowing that the testing of your faith produces Patience

– JAMES 1:3 NKJV

Suffering will produce growth. Many will argue that suffering is unfair because it is designated by Satan but allowed by God. Maturity and growth happen because we are not in control of the circumstance as it relates to time and occurrence. Suffering will make you depend on the faith you developed before the situation arose.

Suffering has a way of driving people closer to God or making them question His actions and being. We will get bitter or grow stronger, and in some cases, we will do both. Suffering will drive you to seek the Savior like the woman with the issue of blood for twelve years described in Mark 5:25-34. Suffering will help you develop patience that you did not think you were capable of displaying. The text in Mark 5:26 says the woman suffered many things from physicians. Let's be clear, this is not a slam on doctors who practice modern medicine. It only displays the point that the woman endured so much in her quest to be made well.

I will briefly tell you about my mother who suffered for many years with numerous health conditions. It started when she was born as a tiny, premature baby. As an adult, she was involved in a severe bus wreck and received extensive back injuries. In her middle age, she was diagnosed with fibromyalgia, COPD, bipolar depression, bone-on-bone rubbing in her hips and shoulders, compressed disk in her back in the L4 and L5 region, and finally, she was diagnosed with chronic lymphatic lymphoma. I saw her suffer day after day with these illnesses. She took fifteen pills in the morning, eight at lunch, and twelve after dinner. She suffered. In her last years, she required eight liters of oxygen. However, she did the best she could to get up each day and get going. Through the pain, I saw her smile when she could. If the grandchildren called or visited, she smiled. Also, if she saw the great-grandchildren, she lit up. Suffering is bearing unspeakable pain. In the end, she fought hard, but she succumbed to COVID compounded with the other illnesses.

I tell this story because you may still be developing your theological view of suffering. Suffering over long periods breaks you down, it breaks your will. Suffering has a way of becoming your identity. Well, I apologize for being morbid, but God knows what we can manage. Each day when I saw my mom, I saw someone struggling to find a higher purpose for which to live.

Suffering will develop your spiritual muscles as you navigate the internal pain you endure. Suffering, as well, drains you mentally and emotionally and you will wonder when this nightmare will end. Mental suffering is something to be discussed and considered today because we have so many individuals facing this situation. To understand how we grow, we must understand that God uses the suffering we face to make us stronger, and it is with this strength that we are able to move in our purpose. This purpose includes our suffering because those situations have formed our character.

Again, I believe that suffering has a higher purpose. However, the question still remains, how can a good God allow bad things to happen to good people? The answer is complicated on many levels. We must remember that everyone has free will and can make whatever decision they wish as it relates to criminal behavior. Individuals choose to hurt others for no apparent reason.

Next, we must consider that God could stop all evil, but He chooses not to because there are "laws of nature" that take place once an event occurs. We must also take into consideration the fact that God did not invent evil. Man invented evil once he knew what evil was. Please remember, God could stop all evil because He is all powerful and all knowing. However, He chooses not to because evil is a part of our system of right and wrong and because we were given free will after the fall of Adam and Eve in the garden.

We must also consider scenarios of natural evil that include hurricanes, tornadoes, earthquakes, floods, and other catastrophic events. Is God responsible? Some would say yes, and others would say no, but the question still remains about the existence and goodness of God. God may allow certain types of evil to draw us closer to Him. Evil and suffering may exist to make us appreciate the good. Suffering may play a greater purpose than we understand. Should the mom of a newborn refrain from getting her baby vaccinated knowing the pain or suffering that will be caused? Or does she reason that the immediate pain of the shot has a greater purpose to keep the baby protected from future sickness?

In 1 Peter 1:7, it is spoken that our faith is "more precious than gold" after we are tested. God in His infinite wisdom knows how much the human spirit can endure before breaking. Suffering makes us stronger if we continue to trust God. Suffering serves as a measure of maturity because we grow deeper in our faith and appreciation for our deliverance. Suffering makes us sensitive to the afflictions of others.

Next, we must understand that God does not allow suffering now so that He can reward us later. He allows suffering now to make us turn to Him and rely on His mighty power for deliverance. He also, in many cases, delivers us now from numerous things. Have you ever wondered about all the negative things that could have happened but did not? I am thankful for His grace and deliverance.

In the end, I believe that suffering is redemptive and has a greater meaning. By this, I mean, as the Scriptures state in 2 Corinthians 4:17, that "our light affliction, which is but for a moment, is working for us a far more exceeding and eternal weight of glory" (NKJV). God has His purposes for His actions, and we will not understand His reasoning because we are not God. With this in mind, suffering can stand to strengthen and mature our faith. Finally, I apologize for the limited information on suffering. I realize that so much more can be said, but time and space do not permit.

15

Transformation

*Be transformed by the renewing of
your mind*

– ROMANS 12:2 NKJV

Transformation is the continuous long game by which Christians grow. In the end, Christians are to strive toward maturity. Spiritual maturity is the after-product of continual growth. As Christians, maturity is thinking like Christ. It is to develop a Christlike approach to your decision-making and daily living. Transformation carries the idea of a caterpillar in a cocoon developing from the inside out. The cocoon is the development place. The cocoon is where the caterpillar is changed into a butterfly. The process is not easy, but growth occurs over time.

As Christians, we mature when the circumstances for growth are present. The above image paints a vivid picture of how change occurs. Change occurs when we allow God to work His divine process in us. Transformation or spiritual change will open doors for ministry based on the fact that God can use your testimony. In addition, transformation means to change after being with God. As people of God, we change after being with Christ. He infuses us with life, goodness, peace, self-control, and discernment. Transformation is the maturing process where God impresses His knowledge into our psyche. Each Christian should allow God to manage their life. The process of spiritual transformation is a slow one where the believer, in concert with God, allows the Holy Spirit the freedom to rule and reign. In spiritual transformation, we change from one form to another, like the caterpillar. We move from sinning more to sinning less due to the changes that are taking place. Transformation requires that we move from the darkness of sin to children of light.

As transformed Christians, we behave differently because the Holy Spirit dwells in us (1 Corinthians 6:19). Maturity is an outgrowth of being transformed by the mighty power of Jesus. The Scriptures extol us to be transformed by the renewing of our minds (Romans 12:2). The word here for renewing is a powerful one. It means to move from one stage to a higher one. It implies that we should be becoming better on an upward continuum. Growth toward Christ is a process with many layers. Christians should want to grow and mature into a vessel that can be leveraged for God. Spiritual maturity is living a renewed life that reflects Jesus and His divine Kingdom. In the end, God does the transforming, and He wants us to draw near to Him through His word. Spiritual maturity is the byproduct of a transformation situation because it leads us to be further shaped to the image of Christ. Mature Christians begin to think differently over time due to the relationship that they develop with God. The relationship grows deeper over time and the Christian begins to trust God more and more.

Transformation is important because the believer allows space for God to inhabit his or her daily life. During the pandemic, I preached a sermon that covered the process of transformation. As many of you know, or will come to know, I am a prop preacher. I use props to illustrate the point to a greater degree. The Holy Spirit gave me a powerful notion early on that Sunday morning. I ran to Walmart and found a Transformer toy. It was cool. It was yellow. It was a Camaro. During the sermon, I pulled out the car to show the audience, and they looked at it strangely. So, I pressed a little further with the example and began to reconfigure the car into a robot. The audience saw the picture. The example was a hit.

Transformation is like that—God literally reconfigures our walk. Yahweh in the person of the Holy Spirit walks beside and inside us to help us change for the best. Transformation is a process where we work with God to comply to His agenda. Spiritual maturity is the byproduct of allowing God to mold us into the image of His dear Son. Let's be clear, we don't have to change, we should want to change to receive the bountiful blessings that are stored up for us. Without transformation, we limit the blessings of peace, love, joy, hope, and self-control that are pending.

Maturing in God is the ultimate show of respect and reverence that worship demands. Generally speaking, it does not take God forever to begin His transformation process; He is specifically waiting on us to surrender and submit, as we discussed in an earlier chapter. One of our greatest problems as agents of free will is the fact that we are rebellious in our nature, which prevents God from fully pouring provision into our lives. However, as Paul found out while on the road to Damascus, he would give God his full attention after God interrupted his travel plans to go and harass and harm other Christians (Acts 9).

My point is this, God can, and He possesses the power to, suddenly change your direction. However, He gave us free choice with the hope that we would want to serve Him out of a changed heart. Transformation requires that we follow God out of obedience and desire rather than out of obligation. In summary, spiritual maturity is where we trust the processes of God to bring us out of the darkness of our selfishness. Transformation is all about yielding to the hand of God as He shapes and reshapes us for His glory.

CHAPTER
16

Growth through Worship

God is Spirit, and those who worship Him must worship in spirit and truth

– JOHN 4:24 NKJV

Worship is a key element in your spiritual growth and maturity. Worship is essential because it honors God. Worship is where we as Christians choose to honor and reverence God for the general goodness of who He is. Every Christian should spend time daily in awe of God for the greatness of His character because of His unfailing love for us.

Psalms 136:1 has a familiar refrain that states, "Oh, give thanks to the LORD, for He is good! For His mercy endures forever." This is a statement of worship because it is a declaration of His powerful attributes of mercy and kindness. The word "thanks" as it relates to worship is underrated in the minds of Christians today. We should be thanking God on a daily basis. In fact, we should thank God minute by minute and hour by hour. Thanksgiving is an element in worship because it sends praise in the direction of God and He appreciates our remembering His greatness. Please know, He does not need our worship from the perspective of obligation. He wants us to praise His mighty name out of sincere desire.

Spiritual maturity is consistently doing the right things over time so it becomes second nature. Worship displays growth and then maturity because we honor God in the fashion that He desires. Maturity enters the equation because we begin to realize that worship is not about us, it is about God. Maturity is knowing this and bringing our best on Sunday or the first day of the week (Acts 20:7). Spiritual maturity requires that we worship on Sunday, which is our official day of worship in the New Testament. The apostles set this in place in 1 Corinthians 16:2 and Acts 20. In fact, we adopt this day in view of the resurrection of Christ from the grave as seen in John 20:1. Sunday replaced the Sabbath for Christians as the day for worship because we are not under the old covenant (Colossians 2:14). Worship requires that we fully serve and pay homage to God because He is the ultimate source of strength.

Next, I submit to you that our worship should extend beyond Sunday in that we should worship God all week long. Let's be clear, Sunday is the official time where we gather to sing, pray, fellowship, commune, give, and hear the Word preached or taught. However, God wants more than one day a week. What if He only blessed us with air one day a week? What if He only let us have use of our eyes or hands once a week? I think you get the point. Worship moves from growth to maturity when we recognize God for His continued faithfulness.

Spiritual maturity is giving God the honor due His name on a daily basis. We do this by living a life that reflects His character. Worship is reflected in our priorities. God expects us to put Him first in our daily actions (Matthew 6:33). Our actions tell it all—what we value most we make a priority. God is not interested in the leftover time that we find for Him at the end of a long day or week. Worship in the course of daily actions includes thinking about God and reflecting on His Word. Worship is praying to God because He wants us to share our intimate thoughts and feelings with Him. Worship is reading and studying the Bible or spiritual principles. This shows God that we are concerned about growing closer to Him.

Spiritual maturity is remembering to humbly seek God on a daily basis. Worship also includes being in a state of deep humility toward God. In this case, we come to rely less on us and more on Him and His goodness. The humility portion of worship is where we prostrate or bow down before a king or someone of great importance. God is the most important being that we know.

Spiritual maturity demands that we not worship ourselves or the accomplishments that we have accumulated. God wants us to serve in a pleasing manner that recognizes Him for His genuine love and care for us. God wants our all, He is not a halfway-do-it type of God. God is a jealous God, but not out of spite or revenge. God is this way because He doesn't like when we replace Him with idols and other things that have no eternal worth.

In John 4:24, we are encouraged to worship God "in spirit and truth." What does this mean, and what does it require? First, let's look at the context. Jesus had just met a woman at a well in the daytime. She was there all alone. Based on her lifestyle, she possibly could not gather water with the rest of the honorable women in the community in the early morning hours because they would look at her differently because of her numerous marriages. Jesus talked to this woman and asked her to give Him a drink, which was not the custom of the day because of her living situation and spiritual condition. The conversation moved to living water and then to true worship. True worship is worshiping in spirit and truth.

For the sake of time, I am not able to explore all the great teaching points from this passage. However, one thing is clear: Jesus wants true worship. True worship is an honest approach to God. True worship is a spiritual declaration that you will humbly approach God with an open heart and mind. Truth is sincerity before God on a daily basis with confession and repentance.

Next, the spiritual part of worship is where we work through the traditions that cause us to serve God robotically. God desires that we freely worship Him out of a willing heart. In the end, worship is where we come honestly before God in recognition that He is our ultimate Maker and Sustainer. Worship is where we surrender praises to God based on His divine goodness.

Worship is where we truthfully bring praises into His presence in a thankful way that honors God.

CHAPTER

17

Forgiveness

And be kind to one another, tenderhearted, forgiving one another, even as God in Christ forgave you

– EPHESIANS 4:32 NKJV

Spiritual maturity will require you to forgive actions from church people and family members. Forgiveness may be one of the toughest things for a Christian to navigate. Trust me, you will be challenged in this area. I know I surely have been. As the old saying goes, "There is no hurt like church hurt." This idiom is true. Yes, that is a core fact. Forgiveness or lack of will stare you in the face until you decide to do something about it. And make no mistake, Satan wants you to live with all the hurt and past feelings that will keep you bound with chains and shackles.

In truth, we know what we should do. In the next few lines, I am going to attempt to appeal to your soul. I hope the Scriptures will appeal to your soul and I hope the examples will tap into that deep space where you may be harboring all that hurt and pain. Forgiveness means to release or let go of something. Forgiveness carries the idea that we allow the account to be settled. In forgiveness, we refuse to hold the weight or the grudge, even though the incident was severe. Forgiveness is letting, or allowing, God to manage His work for your sake. Forgiveness frees you. I will repeat it one more time—forgiveness works to set us free because it releases the grudge, the pain, or the person.

First, we know the Scriptures from beginning to end so I will only mention a few. In Matthew 18:22, we are encouraged to forgive seventy times seven, which indicates an unlimited number. Jesus was ushering in a new law and a new perspective about how His Kingdom would operate. Jesus was exceeding the standard that was used in the Old Law, which was to forgive up to seven times.

Again, we know the Scriptures, but the problem lies in the hurt and the pain we feel because we have been severely wronged, and the person seems to go on existing like nothing has happened. This can make us angry because we may want them to suffer in a small way. However, this is not the way of God. My best example may be the example of Jesus on the cross after the unfair trials, brutal beatings, and the nails being placed in His hands and feet. His statement was, "Father, forgive them; for they know not what they do" (Luke 23:34 KJV). I know you are saying: this was Jesus, a divine man who could have called angels to His side for redemption. Deep in the recesses of my mind I am beginning to think that if He could make it through that, then we can and will make it through our struggles with forgiveness. Please hear me clearly, I am not minimizing your incident, your pain, or your unspeakable horrors. I am hoping that you will one day find the strength of Jesus to help you forgive and move forward. Again, I know you may be hurting, but forgiving is a sign of spiritual growth and maturity. It is the power of God that we may need to rely on to ease the pain.

In addition, spiritual counseling may also need to be considered if you truly want to be healthy. I am also reminded of another example, and it brings up the idea that unforgiveness is like drinking a poison, while hoping the other person gets sick. Do you see it? You are drinking the poison, but you are hoping the other person becomes ill. Rather, we become ill. I only use that example because I want you to mature and become better because you can only control yourself and what you think and how you choose to operate.

A lack of forgiveness is not a good place to be, and I know there are some factors that I am not aware of that have happened. I am writing you this note of encouragement to let you know that the only thing you can do is to rise with purpose each day and give them and the situation over to God. He has the healing power. He has the transforming power. However, we must let Him manage the affairs of the world because He says, "Vengeance is Mine" (Romans 12:19). As you can see, this is a tough subject where we are vulnerable. If possible, pray on a daily basis for the Lord to remove the pain. You will need to repeat this process over and over.

Next, I would like to walk beside you to let you know that the next person who may require forgiving is you. Yes, you. As Christians, we may need to forgive ourselves for failed marriages, wayward children, ill words, horrible attitudes, mood swings, and bad decisions in moments of crisis. Spiritual maturity is where we rely on the power of God to move us forward. This is where the mature Christian says, "Enough is enough. I have punished myself far too long." I am reminded of Romans 8:1 where Paul states that there is "no condemnation to those who are in Christ Jesus" (NKJV). Did you just hear what I heard? We are forgiven and there is no penalty of sin still oppressing us. The problem is that we must believe it.

In summary, I know this is a tough subject, but I wanted to give someone a word of hope to let them know that God will work through any situation if we would only turn it, or them, over to Him.

CHAPTER

18

The Beginning

Whatever things are of good report, if there is any virtue and if there is anything praiseworthy, meditate on these things

– PHILIPPIANS 4:8 NKJV

This chapter is stationed at the end of the book as a way to complete the book on a great note. With that said, this is not a farewell ending. This is a beginning where we begin to believe God at His Word for growth and maturity. In this book, I have attempted to treat those two terms with equal distinction. However, they coincide and work together to bring us to the task of spiritual maturity.

The church is in an uneasy place after COVID-19. Some churches will close, some will merge, and others will thrive because they have come to realize that church growth lies within the people because we are the church. The time is now to edify and build up the saints. This will cause immense growth because

God wants Christians to grow in order to reflect more of His mighty presence.

I am reminded of the time when, after I had preached a sermon, an older gentleman approached me and said, "Preacher, you *hoped* me today." I stood back and realized that, even though his grammar may have been wrong as it related to academics, his intent was well served. Hope is what I want to bring you with this brief work. We all share a hope in Christ, no matter our religious affiliation. It is my hope that you will read this book again and again and pass it along to someone else who wants to experience growth and maturity. Remember, growth leads to spiritual maturity because we are being transformed on a daily basis by the mighty hand and power of Jesus.

Yes, this is a beginning and I thought I would feel some great exhilarating force once the book was completed. I am ever mindful and humble that if I sell only one copy, I have done my job. I just want you to grow and mature in His Word, like kudzu, because if you know anything about it, it is a wild growing vine that takes over everything it touches. Simply stated, it is my earnest prayer that the chapters on transformation, prayer, study, surrender, fasting, desiring God, and discernment will pierce your soul to make you want a deeper relationship with God. I hope you experience God in His awesomeness in your newfound respect for quiet time. I am praying that you will find the power to forgive, as discussed in Chapter 17. In addition, my prayer is that you will grow stronger as you get over your hinderances and sins as you are led by God.

In summary, I hope that you allow the power of the Holy Spirit to rule and reign in your heart forever and ever. I end with an old prayer that I heard as I grew up in a small church in Tennessee. "Now may the sweet communion of the Holy Spirit rest, rule, and abide in you henceforth and forevermore – Amen."

Made in the USA
Monee, IL
18 July 2023